TANKS ILLUSTRATED NO. 8

TANKS ILLUSTRATED NO. 8

US BATTLE TANKS TODAY

STEVEN J. ZALOGA & MICHAEL GREEN

ARMS AND ARMOUR PRESS

London – Melbourne – Harrisburg. Pa. – Cape Town

Introduction

Tanks Illustrated 8: US Battle Tanks Today
Published in 1984 by
Arms and Armour Press, Lionel Leventhal Limited,
2–6 Hampstead High Street, London NW3 1QQ;
4–12 Tattersalls Lane, Melbourne, Victoria 3000,
Australia; Sanso Centre, 8 Adderley Street, P.O. Box 94,
Cape Town 8000; Cameron and Kelker Streets, P.O. Box
1831, Harrisburg, Pennsylvania 17105, USA

British Library Cataloguing in Publication Data:
Zaloga, Steven J.
US battle tanks today. – (Tanks illustrated; 8)
1. Tanks (Military science) – United States – Pictorial
Works
I. Title II. Green, Michael III. Series
623.74'752'0973 UG 446.5
ISBN 0-85368-627-0

Edited by Michael Boxall.
Layout by Roger Chesneau.
Typeset by CCC, printed and bound in Great Britain by
William Clowes Limited, Beccles and London.

The US Army is currently undergoing a major modernization of its tank force, gradually retiring many of its older types manufactured in the 1950s and 1960s, and welcoming a crop of new types, most notably the M1 Abrams. Both the M60A2 and M551A1 have largely gone from the force as a result of prolonged problems with the revolutionary 152mm gun/missile system they both shared. Improvements in ordnance and fire-control technology have given newer tanks like the M1 and M60A3 the high accuracy and high lethality which once could be achieved only by expensive and complex missile systems.

The M60 soldiers on, and will remain numerically the most important US tank type for the next decade. The current fleet is made up mainly of the M60A1 (RISE Passive) type, which incorporates many engine and fire-control improvements, and the M60A3 (TTS) which has a laser range-finder and thermal night-imaging system added. Other improvements are likely over the next few years, including a longer main gun tube to increase the power of the current kinetic energy anti-tank rounds. Another old-timer is the M48, still in service as the M48A5.

The highlight of the US tank force is undoubtedly the M1 Abrams. Although it has been the subject of considerable, and in the authors' view, unwarranted, controversy, its deployment with the Army has gone smoothly. The M1's main advantage over the previous generation of tanks is in terms of mobility and protection. The M1 is the first US tank with Chobham armour, which is virtually impenetrable in the frontal and side quadrants by most Soviet anti-tank rockets, anti-tank missiles and tank HEAT rounds. The new armour is backed up by ammunition compartmentalization and fire-suppression systems to further enhance its survival on the deadly modern battlefield. More obvious is the M1's tremendous speed. It is capable of more than 40mph in terrain, compared to barely 15mph for the M60A1 and most other battle tanks. Speed is important not only in making the tank a more difficult target, but in enabling tank battalions to move swiftly and exploit gaps in enemy lines. The trusty 105mm gun is retained, but from 1985 the M1A1 will be fielded, which shares the same 120mm as the German Leopard 2.

The authors are grateful to many friends for providing photographs. Thanks go to Pierre Touzin, Midic Castelletti, Brian Gibbs, Arnold Meisner, Ron Foulks, George Balin, Jim Loop and Paul Woolf for their help. The authors would also like to thank the tankers of the 2nd Armored Division, 1/149th Armored and 1st Cavalry Division for their hospitality while photographing at Fort Hood and Camp Roberts. Special thanks go to Colonel Bill Highlander of Army Public Affairs for his frequent help; the Public Affairs Office of Aberdeen Proving Grounds and Jim Allingham. The authors would especially like to note the help of Major Geishauser, Major Albro and Lieutenant Coletti of the Public Affairs Office of Fort Hood.

Steven Zaloga and Michael Green, 1984

1. (Title spread) An M48A5 of the original production type. This version retains the commander's cupola and G305 turret vision riser of the old M48A3. (M. Green)
2. A platoon of M60A1s of the 3/63rd Armored on the prowl in Germany, 1973. (Brian Gibbs)

3. The M1 was first deployed with the 1st Cavalry at Fort Hood, Texas in 1981. It saw its first serious tactical trials during 'Operation Reforger' in Germany in September 1982 with the 3rd (Mech) Infantry Division. Here, an M1 of the 64th Armored, 3rd Infantry on the move to the Grafenwoehr training ranges in February 1982. (US Army)

▲4

4. Tank traffic is seen frequently on the autobahns in Germany. Here, an M1 of 64th Armored is seen near the Hohenfels training area. In transit, the M1 usually has its turret traversed rearward and locked. (US Army)

5. A company of M1 tanks of the 64th Armored in February 1982. The tanks are laden with the crews' bedrolls and other personal stores.

6. An M1 in action during 'Operation Reforger' in September 1982. During the exercises, the three battalions of the 64th Armored demonstrated that the M1's high speed was an

important tactical asset in outmanoeuvring opposing tank and mechanized units. (Pierre Touzin)

7. An M1 of 64th Armored during 'Reforger'. This tank is still in mint condition, and has none of the minor field modifications that have since become popular on the M1. (Pierre Touzin)

8. An M1 on manoeuvres in Germany with the 64th Armored in the summer of 1983. The tubular object on the turret side is an ammunition packing tube which is widely used on M1s to store personal equipment outside the tank without getting it wet. (M. Green)

▼5

6▲

7▲ 8▼

▲9

▲10

◀11

9. The high speed of the M1 can lead to epic mudbaths for the crew, especially the driver! (M. Green)

10. The M1 emerges on to dry land. This Abrams belongs to the 64th Armored, stationed in Germany with the 3rd Infantry. (M. Green)

11. An M1 dries off after a mudbath. This view illustrates the standard modification being carried out on the M1's skirt armour. A section has been removed to prevent mud from packing up between the rear drive sprocket and the rear skirt. This skirt, unlike the forward skirt, is unarmoured, so no harm is done by cutting it away. (M. Green)

12. The commander of 1/67th Armored, 2nd Armored Division, LTC Hixson, inspects his tanks prior to exercises. The tanks of this particular battalion are not camouflaged but finished simply in overall forest green. (S. Zaloga)

13. An M1 of 1/67th Armored on tactical exercise in July 1983 at Fort Hood, Texas. An M1 tank platoon consists of four tanks. Here, two (upper right) move out, while the others remain in overwatch position to cover their advance. (S. Zaloga)

12▲ 13▼

▲14

▲15 ▼16

4. An M1 of 1/67th Armored in overwatch position behind an earth berm during tactical exercises. This view clearly illustrates the standard cutaway skirts on operational M1s. (S. Zaloga)
5. An M1 of 1/67th Armored behind a protective berm. Tankers re trained to seek out those terrain features that add to their ank's protection when maintaining a static overwatch of their ellows. (S. Zaloga)
6. The flat prairies of central Texas make excellent tank training rounds. The base at Fort Hood is the largest in the United States, nd is home for more than two armoured divisions. Shown

here, an M1 on one of the ranges. (S. Zaloga)
17. A tank in hull defilade exposes only its thick turret armour to opposing forces. This M1 is battened down for firing. Note that the commander's hatch behind the M2 machine-gun is left partly opened, affording all-around view, while giving the tank commander overhead protection. (S. Zaloga)
18. A platoon of M1s from the 3/67th Armored 'The Hounds of Hell' on a tactical exercise at Fort Hood in July 1983. Their guns are trained on alternate sides of the road to deal with possible ambush by OPFOR training units. (S. Zaloga)

▲19 ▼20

19. The crew of an M1 of 3/67th Armored refuelling from an M559 'Goer' 2,500gal truck. While moving across country at speed, the M1 consumes 5 gallons of jet fuel per mile! (S. Zaloga)
20. An M1 at rest before field exercises. The high speed of the M1 inevitably means that by the end of the day, the tank's rear is entirely caked in mud and dust which provides unintended natural camouflage. (S. Zaloga)
21. The crew of a headquarters tank of 1/67th Armored prepares to move out. A current M1 battalion has two M1 tanks in the HQ platoon and four companies of fourteen M1 tanks each. (S. Zaloga)

21 ▼

▲ 22

▲ 23

22. The business end of the M1. The device above the gun bore is part of the muzzle reference system which is used to determine barrel warp caused by the heat stress of repeated firing. This system feeds its information to the fire-control computer which adjusts the main armament in order to compensate for these effects. (S. Zaloga)

23. An M1 near an ammo dump. The M1 can carry 55 rounds of 105mm ammunition. (S. Zaloga)

24. An M1 of 3/67th Armored, 2nd Armored Division at Fort Hood. The triangular insignia on the turret stowage box is used as a divisional insignia at Fort Hood to distinguish tanks of the 2nd Armored Division from those of the neighbouring 1st Cavalry. Evident on the side of the vehicle are the battalion tactical insignia, preceded by a black 'Hounds of Hell' silhouette. (S. Zaloga)

25. An M1 of Company C, 3/67th Armored. This view clearly shows the battalion insignia used by this unit which refers back to the battalion's traditional name. (S. Zaloga)

24▼

25▼

▲26 ▼27

28▲

26. M1s of 3/67th Armored in the battalion motor-pool preparing for night tactical exercises. The tanks are to be fuelled and loaded with ammunition for live firing. (S. Zaloga)

27. This view of an M1 of 3/67th Armored highlights the low, sleek lines of the tank. (S. Zaloga)

28. Tankers from 1/67th Armored prepare the commander's M2 .50cal machine-gun and the loader's M240 7.62mm machine-gun. It will be noted that when outside the tank, members of the crew usually wear a 'steel pot' rather than the CVC tanker's helmet which are usually stowed outside the tank when in action. (S. Zaloga)

29. A platoon of M1s from 3/67th Armored move out to the firing ranges. (S. Zaloga)

29▼

30. Final inspection before an M1 platoon departs the battalion motor-pool for field manoeuvres. The rubber dust-covers have yet to be removed from the main gun tubes. (S. Zaloga)

31. Although the M1 is a good deal lower than the older M60, its turret is quite massive as is evident in this view. The large size is due mainly to the thick armour. The M1 is in fact smaller inside than the M60. (S. Zaloga)

32. A tanker from 2nd Armored Division prepares a HEAT training round for the M1. Gone are the days of brass ammunition casings, aluminium having taken their place. A round like this weighs about 50 pounds and has to be handled with care. (S. Zaloga)

33. A close-up of the commander's station on the M1. The M2 .50cal machine-gun can be fired from outside the hatch, or can be remote-controlled from within the tank. (S. Zaloga)

30 ▶

▼31

32 ▲ 33 ▼

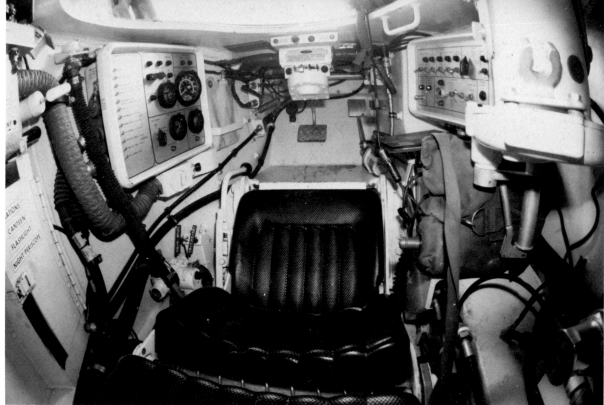

▲34

34. The driver's station in the M1. Because of the shallow angle of the bow armour, the driver is almost flat on his back. His main control is the steering device in the upper centre of the picture. The steering arms are much like the handle bars of a motorcycle, and are remarkably simple to use once the driver has got the feel of a tank capable of 40mph. Careless driving at high speed tends to hurl the turret crew around a bit! (S. Zaloga)

▼35

35. The fighting compartment of the M1. In front is the gunner and behind him, the tank commander (TC). The TC's sights are integrated with the gunner's sights, so the usual procedure is for the TC to select a target with his sights and roughly aim the turret towards the target. The gunner then fine aims the gun which is fully stabilized, allowing it to be accurately aimed even when the vehicle is moving across country at top speed. (S. Zaloga)

36 ▲

36. A view from the TC's station. To the left is the gun breech and the gun loader. Forward is the TC's sight and the gunner's station. The latter is equipped with both conventional day-optics and a thermal night sight which requires no artificial or starlight illumination. (S. Zaloga)

37. A view from the loader's station towards the TC's station, showing the specially armoured doors behind which the ammunition is stored. If the ammunition compartment were penetrated, the doors would protect the crew from ammunition fires or blasts which would be ducted upward through panels in the turret roof. The doors are easily operated by the gunner's knee so that he can keep his hands free to handle the heavy ammunition. (S. Zaloga)

37 ▼

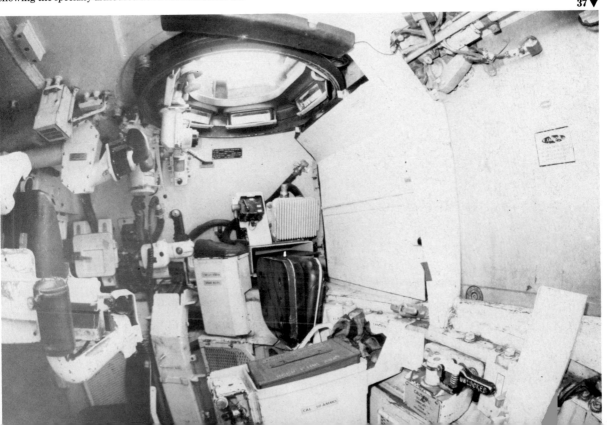

38. Sergeant Herring of the 2nd Armored Division in the loader's position of the M1. A few rounds are stowed in ready racks in front of the gunner, but most are located in the rear turret bustle behind specially armoured doors. (S. Zaloga)
39. M1 tanks of the 2nd Armored Division on tactical exercise at Fort Hood, Texas, 1983. (S. Zaloga)
40. An M1 of the 2nd Armored Division, Fort Hood, 1983.
41. (Next spread) The tremendous horsepower of the M1 Abrams is evident in this view at Aberdeen Proving Grounds. (S. Zaloga)

▼**38**

▲42 ▼43

42. M1 Abrams tanks of the 3/67th Armored 'Hounds of Hell' at Fort Hood, 1983. (S. Zaloga)
43. M1 of 1/67th Armored at Fort Hood, with a smoke round going off in the background. (S. Zaloga)
44. One of the reasons for the greatly increased accuracy of modern tank guns is this inconspicuous little muzzle reference system. The device beams a signal to the gunner's sight which provides information on barrel warp. The signal is transmitted to the tank's ballistic computer which adjusts the gun angle if

repeated firing has warped the barrel excessively. While seemingly complex, these features have been so well integrated into the fire-control system that the gunner's task in an M1 is much easier than on the older M60A1. (S. Zaloga)
45. The successor to the M1 will be the M1A1 (currently given the experimental designation M1E1). The primary difference between the M1 and the M1E1 is the use of the larger 120mm gun, and there are many internal improvements. (TACOM)

▲46

▲47

46. A rear view of the M1E1, showing the larger turret basket which has been added. (TACOM)

47. The M1E1 is distinguishable from the M1 by the rounded fume extractor on the gun barrel, and the added turret basket at the rear. (TACOM)

48. The M60A2 'Starship' during the 1979 'Reforger' exercise. As its nickname implies, the M60A2 had a very complicated fire-control system. Problems caused by shock damage stemming from use of conventional HE projectiles eventually spelled the end for

this tank which was subsequently retired. Many of the hulls will be converted to special purpose vehicles. In the background is another M60 variant – the M60AVLB assault bridge vehicle. (P. Touzin)

49. 'Eskimo Nell', an M60A1 of 3/63rd Armored in Germany in 1973. The battalion insignia, a knight's head, is evident on the barrel fume extractor. The vehicle's name stems from a bawdy Canadian epic verse, popular among Canadian soldiers. This tank is fitted with the older VSS-2 IR searchlight. (Brian Gibbs)

▲ 50

▲ 51 ▼ 52

50. A pair of 3/63rd Armored's M60A1s on tactical exercise in 1973. This battalion 'liberated' some old M47 tank stowage bins which were attached on the turret rear. The M47 bins were preferred for stowing personal gear since they could be sealed from the damp. (Brian Gibbs)

51. An M60A1 (RISE) during the 1978 'Reforger' exercises in Germany. The small octagonal blocks hanging from the turret basket are replacement shoes for the T142 track. (P. Touzin)

52. A frequent sight in German hamlets during the autumn are NATO tanks lumbering through on the way to mock battles. They are invariably trailed by jeeps which assess and pay for damages caused by the tanks when they inadvertently nudge parked cars and the like. This M60A1 (RISE) is fitted with the new smoke mortar array. (P. Touzin)

53. An M60A1 (RISE Passive) in full 'Reforger' regalia. The temporary manoeuvres markings (62A) in blue or orange reveal which 'Army' the tank belongs to. Just behind the fume extractor on the barrel is a pyrotechnic simulator which is 'fired' at 'hostile' tanks. If an umpire judges a tank to be hit, an amber rotating beacon (bubble-gum machine) is turned on to proclaim the victim. (P. Touzin)

54. An M60A1 (RISE) with dozer attachment of 4/73rd Armored. One tank in each company is fitted with a dozer blade for digging positions for the tanks to conceal themselves in hull defilade. (P. Touzin)

55. The combat engineer version of the M60A1 tank is the M728 CEV. This vehicle has a jib boom for minor repair work, and has a 165mm howitzer for demolishing bunkers and concrete obstructions. (P. Touzin)

53 ▲

54 ▲ 55 ▼

▲56

▲57 ▼58

56. A new M60A3 after init[ial] deployment with 37th Armored in Germany durin[g] the 1982 'Reforger' exercise. The M60A3 can be most readily distinguished by the thermal sleeve around the gu[n] tube. (P. Touzin)

57. An M60A1 (RISE) duri[ng] the 1981 'Reforger' exercise[s in] Germany. Since 1977, US tanks have been retro-fitted with smoke mortars based on [a] British design. (P. Touzin)

58. The crews of these M60[A1] (RISE) tanks are carrying ou[t] preventive maintenance on t[he] tracks during 'Reforger' exercises. The manoeuvres markings are evident despite the turret camouflage. (P. Touzin)

59. A CH-47 Chinook helicopter flies over a pair of M60A1 (RISE) tanks during the 1981 'Reforger' exercise. (P. Touzin)

60. A thoroughly camouflag[ed] M60A1 (RISE Passive) duri[ng] the 1980 'Reforger' exercises. One only hopes that nobody fires the pyrotechnic simulat[or] with all the netting over it! (P. Touzin)

61. An M60A3 of 37th Armored. Although not a standard fit, most M60A1s carry a couple of 5gal oilcans on the rear of the trackguard. (P. Touzin)

59▲

60▲ 61▼

62. A clear view of an M60A3 with a fully-loaded pyrotechnic simulator on the gun barrel. (P. Touzin)
63. An M60A3 crew take a breather next to an M113 of the 4th Infantry during the September 1982 'Reforger' exercise. (P. Touzin)

◀**62** ▼**63**

▲64 ▼65

66▲

64. An M60A3 dozer of 1/37th Armored, with an M151 Mutt in the background. (P. Touzin)
65. An M60A1 (RISE Passive) stationed with the Berlin Brigade in West Berlin. This vehicle is fitted with the newer VSS-3A IR night searchlight. (M. Green)
66. An old M60A1 of the 1st Cavalry Division at Fort Hood in July 1983. The 1st Cavalry has not been equipped with newer

versions of the M60A1 since it will soon be re-equipping entirely with M1 tanks. (S. Zaloga)
67. An M60A1 of the 1st Cavalry. The strip at the very base of the turret is Velcro and is used to attach the detector strip of the MILES laser simulator device which is widely used for tactical training by the US Army. (S. Zaloga)

67▼

▲68

68. An M60A1 (RISE) at the Armor Training Center at Fort Knox, Kentucky in 1982. The crew has found a convenient place on the turret side to dry out their rubber 'muckluck' boots. (M. Green)

69. An M60A1 (RISE) on tactical manoeuvres at the Armor Training Center. The tank has the mounting brackets for the smoke launcher, but the mortar itself is not fitted. (M. Green)

70. The M60A1 (RISE) designation refers to the improved RISE engine installed in this version of the M60A1. Most M60A1s are being rebuilt to M60A1 (RISE) standard. (M. Green)

70▶

▲71

71. An M60A1 (RISE) at the Armor Training Center at Fort Knox. The pyrotechnic simulator has evidently been fired a few times during the day's training. (M. Green)
72. An M60A3 in mint condition at Fort Knox. The added thermal sleeve on the barrel is very clearly seen. (Ron Foulks)
73. An M60A3 at Aberdeen Proving Grounds. This tank is lacking the small rectangular box carried on the turret side for additional smoke mortar rounds. (S. Zaloga)
74. One of the features that distinguish the M60A3 from the

earlier M60A1 is this cross-wind sensor, located at the rear of the turret roof. It provides automatic data up-dates to the tank's ballistic computer, allowing the computer to adjust for cross-winds in the flight-path of the projectile. (S. Zaloga)
75. One of the less noticeable features of the M60A3 is the substitution of a laser range-finder for the older optical range-finder of the M60A1. The laser range-finder has a small oval access port over the optics on the right range-finding dome as seen here. (S. Zaloga)

▼72

73▲ 74▼

75▼

76. One of life's little joys. Repairing an AVDS-1790 diesel in the field. (Brian Gibbs)

77. Another of life's little pleasures – replacing an M60A1's track.

The M60A1 uses 'live' track which accounts for its curling. (Brian Gibbs)

78. Another 2nd Armored Division M1, Fort Hood, 1983.

▲ 79

79. M60A1 (RISE) of the Armor Training Center at Fort Knox, Kentucky. (M. Green)

80. M48A5 Pattons of 1/149th Armor at Camp Roberts, Ky. (M. Green)

▼ 80

81. M551A1s of 4/68th Armored, the last operational M551A1 unit, serving with the 82nd Airborne Division. (US Army)

82. An ersatz Shilka and T-72 of an OPFOR unit at the Desert Training Center in California. (M. Green)

▲ 83 ▼ 84

83. Although not a tank, the Army is planning to acquire the new LAV (Light Armoured Vehicle) for use by special MPG battalions to support light divisions. These are intended for rapid deployment by aircraft to trouble spots around the world and hence special emphasis is placed on light weight. (GM-Canada)

84. Only a single tank battalion, the 4/68th Armored, attached to the 82nd Airborne Division, retains the M551A1 Sheridan for front-line service. (82nd Airborne Public Affairs Department)

85. A view through the loader's hatch of an M60. This was taken inside the turret of the experimental M60AX, but the basic layout is identical with that of an M60A1. (S. Zaloga)

86. E3 Robert Yancey of the 1st Cavalry demonstrates breech operation in an M60A1 tank. The ammunition in the M60A1 is stored in the tubes behind the loader. (S. Zaloga)

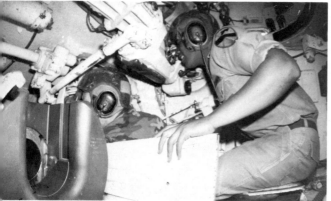
▲87

▲88

▲89

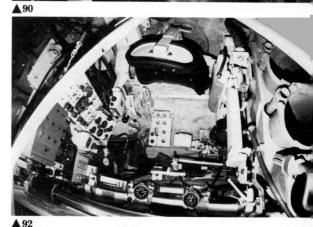
▲90

▲91

▲92

87. The fighting compartment of the M60A1. The gunner sits in the forward portion of the turret, with the commander behind and above him. (S. Zaloga)

88. A view of the turret of an M60A1 from the commander's station. (S. Zaloga)

89. A view of the TC's station and turret rear from the loader's position. As can be seen, ammunition is also stowed below the turret. (S. Zaloga)

90. The gunner's station and sights in the M60A1. The mechanism on the right side of the picture is the hydraulic turret drive. (S. Zaloga)

91. The turret rear of the M60A1 showing ammunition stowage. (S. Zaloga)

92. The driver's station on the M60A1. The M60 employs a very simple steering arm. (S. Zaloga)

93. The M1 commander's cupola on the M60A1 tank. The usual M85 .50cal machine-gun has not been fitted. (S. Zaloga)

93 ▶

94. ▲

94. The short 165mm howitzer of the M728 CEV is very evident in this view of an engineer tank of the 2nd Armored Division. (S. Zaloga)

95. The ROBAT is a remote-controlled minefield clearing vehicle based on surplus M60A2 hulls. Apart from the mine roller attachment, the ROBAT is fitted with a mine-clearing charge in the container on the roof. A rocket propels the long hose charge over the minefield, where it is detonated. This frees a path wide enough for tanks to pass safely. (MERADCOM)

95. ▼

▲96

97▲

96. The standard assault bridge of the US Army is the M60 AVLB, mounted on an M60A1 chassis. It is used for crossing anti-tank ditches, obstacles and small obstructions. (P. Touzin)

97. Besides the standard M60 AVLB, MERADCOM is also developing a longer heavy assault bridge, carried on an M60 hull. (MERADCOM)

98. An M60A1 firing at night. The flight-path of the projectile is visible because of the tracer, used at the base of all tank rounds. (Brian Gibbs)

◄98

▲ 99

99. The M60AX, also called the Super M60, is a privately developed improved M60A1 with special spaced armour. It was developed by Teledyne Continental, and was demonstrated to the US Marines, who currently use the M60A1. (Teledyne Continental)

100. M48A5 tanks of 1/102nd Armored, 50th Armored Division, move out of the motor-pool at Camp Drum, New York, on summer exercises. (M. Castelletti)

101. The 50th Armored Division, like most National Guard tank units, is equipped entirely with the M48A5. Most of the Jersey Blues' tanks are the later M48A5 (Low Profile) type with the smaller Urdan, commander's cupola and externally-mounted M60 machine-guns. (M. Castelletti)

100 ▶

101 ▼

▲102

102. M48A5 (Low Profile) of the 1/102nd Armored on the firing ranges at Camp Drum. (M. Castelletti)
103. A camouflaged M48A5 of the 1/149th Armored at Camp Roberts in California. In contrast to the 1/102nd Armored, the 1/149th have their tanks camouflaged in desert rather than temperate colours. (M. Green)
104. This close-up shows the roof of the later-production M48A5

(Low Profile). The smaller, commander's cupola is based on the cupola used on the original M48, and was manufactured by Urdan in Israel; a rare example of US military equipment acquisition from Israel. (George Balin)
105. In front of their M48A5, a tank crew from 1/149th Armored takes a breather during summer exercises. (M. Green)

▼103

▲106

106. An M48A5 (Low Profile) in the motor-pool of 1/149th Armored. This unit traces its roots back to the old California 40th Tank Company which in turn formed a part of the Provisional Tank Group which was the first US tank unit to see combat during the Second World War, in the Philippines in 1941. (M. Green)

107. The M48A5 is usually fitted with the older VSS-2 infra-red searchlight. (M. Green)

108. The M60 machine-gun fitted to the M48A5 (Low Profile) is clearly silhouetted in this view of California National Guard tanks. (M. Green)

109. An M48A5 dozer of 1/149th Armored. (M. Green)

110. A camouflaged M48A5 (Low Profile) with an M113 in the background. In tank battalions, the M113s are used as utility and command vehicles. (M. Green)

111. An M48A5 of 1/149th Armored hides on the reverse slope of a hill during summer exercises. (M. Green)

◀107 ▼108

109 ▲

110 ▲ 111 ▼

▲112

◄113

112. An interesting view of an officially non-existent version of the M48A5. All early-model M48A5 tanks are supposed to have the G305 turret riser under the machine-gun cupola, but this vehicle has dispensed with it. (M. Green)

113. This head-on shot of an M48A5 (Low Profile) shows that the M48 retains the old T107 track, rather than the T142 replaceable pad track used on most M60A1s. (M. Green)

114. A heavily-camouflaged M48A5 (Low Profile) lurks on the reverse slope of a hill waiting for a target. This is a standard tanker's trick. To an opponent on the other side of the hill, only the top of the turret will be evident. (M. Green)

115. The original version of the M48A5 used the same .50cal machine-gun as the M48A3. On the M48A5 (Low Profile) tanks, two M60 7.62mm machine-guns have been substituted. (M. Green)

114▲ 115▼

▲116

▲117 ▼118

116. An M48A5 (Low Profile) of B Company, 1/149th Armored lurks under natural cover during manoeuvres. (M. Green)
117. It is sometimes difficult to tell an M48A5 from an M60. In a frontal view, they can be distinguished by the rounded bow of the M48 compared to the straight bow line of the M60. (M. Green)
118. M48A5s of the 1/149th Armored on review after summer manoeuvres. (M. Green)
119. One of the minor changes on the M48A5 (Low Profile) from the earlier models was the addition of screening in the rear external turret baskets to prevent small items of gear from falling out. (M. Green)
120. A pair of early model M48A5s on patrol at Camp Roberts. (M. Green)
121. A little greenery adds some colour to the sand camouflaged M48A5s of 149th Armored. (M. Green)

119▲

120▲ 121▼

123. If an M88 recovery vehicle isn't handy, a string of tanks can be linked to tow a disabled tank out of a ditch as is demonstrated by M48A5s (Low Profile) of 1/102nd Armored of the Jersey Blues. (M. Castelletti)

123 ▼

▲124

124. A little too much rain at Camp Drum can really spoil a tanker's day. An M48A5 (Low Profile) bogged down with a couple of stalwart friends trying to help out. (M. Castelletti)

125. Although the regular tank version of the M551A1 is no longer in widespread service, the M551 serves on with the

OPFOR. OPFORs are training units configured like Soviet units and used to train US combat troops. At the Desert Training Center in California, M551s have been rebuilt to resemble various Soviet tank and armoured vehicle types. In this case, believe it or not, an Amerikansky T-72? (M. Green)

▼125

126 ▲

126. The OPFORs have played a vital role in realistic training of US tank troops. Scoring is done using the MILES laser training devices. Each tank has a 'laser gun' in the barrel which 'fires' at opposing tanks. The fire is picked up by small laser detectors on the target tank, and a kill sets off a smoke grenade and incapacitates the victim tank. More vital than the MILES at the Desert Training Center is the plastic cooler on the engine deck, no doubt full of some delightful liquid brew to refresh the crew. (M. Green)

127. A bunch of diehard OPFOR Reds commanding an ersatz T-72 company, confer at the Desert Training Center. These OPFORs are considerably more skilled at exercises than any units, Soviet or American, and often win the various wargames. (M. Green)

127 ▼

▲128 ▼129

130 ▲

128. The strange barrel on the .50cal machine-gun on the vehicles of this unit is a 'shredder' used when firing .50cal blanks. The blanks have a small wood core which the shredder mangles to prevent it causing injury. (M. Green)
129. While this ersatz T-72 wouldn't fool anybody, it does beat the old method of using M60A1 tanks to simulate hostile tanks! (M. Green)
130. Probably the most convincing of the M551 training tanks is this imitation of a Soviet ZSU-23-4 Shilka. (M. Green)
131. This training tank is presumably intended to represent an SO-152 (2S3) self-propelled howitzer. (M. Green)

131 ▼

▲132

132. A battery of ersatz SO-152s on the move. (M. Green)
133. An impressive show of strength by an OPFOR motor rifle company on the attack. (M. Green)
134. Probably the least convincing of the M551 training tanks is this curious attempt at duplicating a Soviet BMP Korshun. The

imitation Sagger missile looks as if it has seen better days. (M. Green)
135. This ersatz BMP clearly shows the MILES detector strips around the base of the turret used in tactical field exercises at the Desert Training Center. (M. Green)

▼133

▲136

136. Among the light tanks in development is this version of the RDF Light Tank. This is an outgrowth of the HSTV-L experimental light tank developed by AAI Corporation for Army tests. The Army intends to continue to develop light tanks like these to serve as surrogate main battle tanks in support of air-lifted light divisions. (AAI Corpn.)

137. Onward to the West! Forward to Modesto! An ersatz BMP with the commander in a pose reminiscent of Soviet wartime propaganda photographs. (M. Green)

▼137